THE GOVERNMENT ORDER BLUEPRINT

THE GOVERNMENT ORDER BLUEPRINT

Dr. Anujj K Jain

Available on amazonkindle

Worldwide Published by

Pendown Press
PREMIUM BUSINESS PUBLISHER

PENDOWN PRESS LLP
An ISO 9001 & ISO 14001 Certified Co.,
Regd. Office: 3767A, Kanhaiya Nagar,
Tri Nagar, Delhi-110035
Ph.: 8130886000, 9650072927
E-mail: info@pendownpress.com
Branch Office: 1A/2A, 20, Hari Sadan, Ansari Road,
Daryaganj, New Delhi-110002
Ph.: 011-45794768
Website: PendownPress.com

Edition: 2026
Price: ₹ 399
ISBN: 978-93-7217-438-0

Layout and Cover Designed by Pendown Graphics Team

TABLE OF CONTENTS

ACKNOWLEDGEMENTS

No book is ever the effort of one person alone, and this one is certainly no exception. Though my name may appear on the cover, the ideas, persistence, and spirit that made these pages possible are the product of many hands, hearts, and minds. I owe an immeasurable debt of gratitude to those who have stood beside me along this journey.

First and foremost, I thank my parents, who gave me the greatest gifts of all: their unwavering love, their values, and the foundation of curiosity and discipline that shaped me. They instilled in me the importance of hard work, integrity, and compassion; qualities without which this book would never have come into being.

To my wife, whose constant encouragement, patience, and faith in me carried me through the most challenging days. Her intellectual support, her ability to listen and challenge my ideas, and her quiet strength kept me grounded and inspired.

To my children, who fill my life with joy, laughter, and boundless curiosity. Their questions, wonder, and resilience remind me why learning and creating matter so much. They are both my greatest teachers and my happiest distractions.

To my mentors and teachers, who guided me with wisdom, opened doors of understanding, and showed me the power of knowledge and generosity. Their voices echo through these pages.

I would like to extend my heartfelt gratitude to **Akshar Yadav,** whose visionary marketing leadership and deep expertise have been a constant source of inspiration. His insights as a true "Marketing Guru" have helped me think expansively and sharpen my message.

I am equally grateful to **Dr. Rakesh Arya,** my mentor in more ways than one — his wisdom, structured guidance, and unshakeable commitment to personal growth have shaped not only this book, but also my approach to life.

To my friends and extended family, who provided encouragement, companionship, and moments of respite when I needed them most. Their presence reminded me that life is richer when shared.

To my colleagues, whose collaboration, insights, and challenges sharpened my thinking and expanded my perspective. Working alongside them has been a constant source of growth.

I am profoundly grateful to my publisher, Dinesh Verma, CEO of Pendown Press, and his team. Their commendable efforts, steady guidance, and meticulous attention to detail made the editing, writing, and publishing process not only smooth but joyful.

Finally, to you, the reader, thank you for picking up this book. By engaging with these words, you give meaning to the work that has gone into them. I hope these pages offer you something valuable, whether insight, inspiration, or even just a moment of reflection.

This book exists because of all of you.

PREFACE: THE GAME HAS CHANGED

The Government is not a challenge for those who understand its language.
It is an opportunity for those who respect its purpose, align with its energy, and build spaces that foster trust and prosperity."

~ Dr. Anujj K Jain

For decades, Indian businesses believed that success in government projects required connections, influence, or bending the rules. However, today a new path is emerging, a path based on **strategic alignment,** not manipulation.

Over the past decade, India has witnessed a profound shift in its governance culture, making it faster, cleaner, more accessible, and more inclusive for businesses and entrepreneurs. The era of relying on connections, long delays, and opaque dealings is making way for digital-first, results-driven policies and a more accountable administration.

Here are the key improvements that have reshaped the Government–Business landscape:

1. **Digitization of Processes**
   - The introduction of platforms like the Government e-Marketplace (GeM) is making procurement open and online.

- Portals like PFMS (Public Financial Management System) ensure that payments are faster, trackable, and transparent.

2. **Transparent Approvals and Processes**
   - End of manual files and delays with the advent of eOffice and the digital movement of files across departments.
   - RTI is making data access routine and fostering a culture of accountability.

3. **Policy Framework for Entrepreneurship**
   - Launch of Startup India, making it simpler for entrepreneurs and MSMEs to register, access benefits, and participate in government projects.
   - Specific policies for women entrepreneurs, SC/ ST ventures, rural enterprises, and first-generation entrepreneurs.

4. **Focus on Skill Development and Sustainability**
   - Programs like PMKVY, Skill India Mission, and NULM are making skilling mainstream.
   - Greater focus on sustainability and aligning CSR efforts with national priorities.

5. **Outcome-Driven Government**
   - Shift from input-based to outcome-based governance.
   - Government departments openly collaborate with NGOs, entrepreneurs, and social enterprises to achieve measurable results.

6. **Citizen-Centric Governance**
   - Services like MyGov, mobile service delivery platforms, digital grievance redressal, and state dashboards are making governance more inclusive and participatory.
   - Public review of policies and digital town halls is making policymaking more responsive and inclusive.
7. **Ease of Regulations**
   - Reduced compliance burdens for MSMEs.
   - Simplification of GST filings, online licensing, and approvals makes it faster, friendlier, and more accessible to do business.

What this shift means is that the old excuses no longer apply.

- You don't need connections; you need a solid proposal.
- You don't have to wait for tenders; you can build pilots and form direct relationships.
- You don't have to operate in the shadows; you can operate openly, strategically, and with pride.

The New Era: An Invitation to Partner

Today, more than ever, the Government is looking for trusted partners, businesses that can align with national priorities and deliver tangible outcomes.

If you can:

- Speak the language of policy,
- Build results-driven pilots,

- Maintain strong compliance,
- Operate with integrity and accountability,

...you're already well-positioned to win.

The last ten years have laid the foundation for a more inclusive, innovative, and impact-focused Government–Business collaboration.

This book gives you the roadmap not just to adapt, but to thrive in this new era. It is your guide to

- Understanding the language and priorities of Government departments.
- Building long-term, ethical, and outcome-driven collaborations.
- Applying the power of Vaidik Vastu and Energy Transformation to create environments that attract opportunity, foster trust, and enable long-term growth.

Be the Insider, Not the Outsider

If you're reading this, you're not looking for shortcuts. You're looking for **powerful, legal, and predictable ways to grow.**

It's time to stop playing small.

The Government is not slow: your strategy might be.

It's time to change that now.

Bridging the Gap Between Business, Government, Vastu, and Energy

Over three decades of experience have helped me emerge as a trusted advisor for entrepreneurs, NGOs, and institutions seeking to build meaningful, long-term collaborations with the Government of India.

This has been made possible due to a unique blend of deep-rooted knowledge in business strategy, public policy, Vaidik Vastu, and Energy Transformation that allows me to guide leaders to align spaces, energies, and offerings with national priorities, unlocking growth, trust, and abundance.

A New Dimension of Business Growth

This unique approach that blends ancient wisdom and modern strategy has led organizations to:

- Identify hidden opportunities within Government policies and departments.
- Position offerings strategically, making them irresistible to Government stakeholders.
- Leverage Vaidik Vastu and Energy Transformation Techniques to create spaces and workplaces that foster productivity, alignment, and prosperity.

If you're an entrepreneur, changemaker, or institution seeking guidance on Government Engagement, Business Growth, or Energy Optimization, you can connect with me at

✉ **Email:** md@optymystix.com; optymystix@gmail.com

LinkedIn: https://www.linkedin.com/in/dranujjkjain/

CHAPTER 1

THE MYTHS THAT HOLD YOU BACK

For many years, the Indian business landscape has been clouded with myths about government work. Whether it's a small business owner in Tier 2 cities or a mid-sized enterprise in urban India, there's a prevailing sense of mystery, fear, and confusion around government business.

This chapter aims to dismantle the most common misconceptions and bring clarity to entrepreneurs who are serious about playing big, but playing clean.

Myth 1: "Only Big Players Get Government Work"

This belief is deeply ingrained. Business owners often assume that only large corporations, or those with deep political connections, have access to government contracts. While it is true that big players often have more resources to apply for tenders.

The truth is that the government is actively encouraging MSMEs and startups to participate in its procurement processes.

The Indian government has rolled out several inclusive initiatives, such as:

- **Public Procurement Policy for MSEs:** Mandating government departments to procure a minimum percentage from micro and small enterprises.
- **Startup India:** Easing norms, simplifying registration, and opening procurement to innovative young companies.
- **GeM (Government e-Marketplace):** A revolutionary step where even solo entrepreneurs can register and sell to government bodies.

What keeps many businesses out isn't a lack of opportunity; it's a lack of awareness and the belief that the playing field isn't level.

But if you're innovative, compliant, and persistent, you have a place in this ecosystem.

Myth 2: "You Need Setting and Source"

In countless conversations with business owners, this phrase keeps cropping up: "*Woh kaam setting se hota hai*" (that work happens through connections). For decades, this has been the go-to belief that someone sitting in a chair with power must be 'managed' or 'convinced' behind closed doors.

The truth is: the entire system is evolving. Vigilance systems, transparency protocols, file movement tracking, digital audits- these aren't just reforms. They're culture shifts.

Yes, **relationships matter, but not the old-school type.**

Modern government-business relationships are:

- Transparent
- Documented
- Strategic

The new influence is credibility.

- Have you shown thought leadership in your niche?
- Is your business profile visible and clean?
- Do you offer real solutions aligned with a department's mission?

These are your new tools of persuasion.

Myth 3: "Tenders are the Only Way In"

Tenders are visible, yes.

But they are often:

- Overcrowded
- Price-driven
- Time-sensitive

Most people don't know that departments **work on dozens of mandates,** policy goals, development targets, and public pressure, many of which are underfunded or under-resourced.

This is where strategic businesses step in, not to manipulate, but to help departments succeed.

You can:

- Create pilot project proposals aligned with budget allocations
- Offer capacity-building services or training workshops
- Partner under CSR or MoU terms
- Get empanelled for recurring needs

These are proactive, consultative models, not reactive tender-bidding games.

The best part? The field is wide open. Most businesses don't even know this space exists.

Myth 4: "Government Business is Too Slow"

There is some truth here, but the full picture tells a different story.

Why does it feel slow?

- Too much dependency on informal agents
- Incomplete documentation
- Misalignment with internal workflows

But once you understand how departments operate, their workflow, hierarchy, and pain points, things start to move faster.

Especially with digitization initiatives like:

- eOffice
- eTendering
- Online file movement tracking
- PFMS for transparent payments

The reality is: many businesses delay themselves through:

- Poor follow-up
- Ignoring compliance
- Not building rapport with the right nodes

Speed is strategy. You don't speed up the system; you align better with it.

Myth 5: "I Need an Agent to Get Things Done"

This myth is the most dangerous of all, because it leads to:

- Financial loss
- Reputational damage
- Legal risk

The so-called "liaison agents" have built a parallel market. Their pitch is always similar:

- "I know someone inside."
- "I can get the file signed."
- "Give me advance, I'll start the process."

But what you never get is:

- Legal documentation
- Official contracts
- Verifiable credentials

It's time to stop outsourcing your government strategy to these unverified entities. Instead, build:

- Internal capacity
- Relationship capital (the right way)
- Process intelligence

It takes more effort, but it gives you long-term leverage and zero dependency.

Why These Myths Are Dangerous

Beliefs shape decisions. Decisions shape destiny.

The myths we've covered above are not just "wrong ideas";

they're blockers to:

- Confidence
- Credibility
- Capability

They breed:

- Excuses
- Delays
- Missed opportunities

What's worse, they push the honest player out of the game and allow the unethical to thrive.

The Mindset Shift You Need

It all begins in your head.

From:

- "Government is not for me."

To:

- "Government needs people like me."

You are not a vendor. You are a value creator.

Start asking:

- How does my solution align with this department's mandate?
- What KPIs of the ministry does my business directly impact?
- Can I help them do their job better, faster, or cheaper?

This is **strategic service,** not just supply.

Strategic players are not intimidated by the system; they study it. They don't run from officials; they engage with clarity. They don't wait for tenders; they create opportunities.

Kill the Myth, Claim the Market

It all starts with one decision: to stop believing in shortcuts and start believing in strategy.

Every myth you drop clears space for powerful action.

- You don't have to be a big player
- You don't need "source" or "setting"
- You don't have to wait for tenders
- You don't need an agent to succeed
- You don't have to struggle with slow systems

You just need the right map. And that's what the next chapters will give you.

So, are you ready to stop playing small? Because the government isn't slow. **Your strategy might be.** Let's fix that.

Chapter 2

The Hidden Demand Inside Government Departments

The biggest opportunities in business often lie in places others ignore. For most Indian entrepreneurs, government business is seen as a fortress, guarded by bureaucracy, unreachable officers, and outdated systems. But in reality, inside this very system lies a goldmine of hidden demand, consistent, underserved, and often urgent. The smart business owners are not chasing tenders; they are identifying and solving these hidden needs.

This chapter will walk you through:

- How hidden demand in government works
- Where to find it
- How to align your business with it
- How to become the go-to solution provider for departments

1. Understanding the Nature of Government Demand

The Government of India functions not only as a policymaker and regulator but also as the **largest institutional buyer** in the economy. Whether through central ministries, state departments, district administrations, or autonomous bodies, it requires an unending supply of services, solutions, and innovations.

However, **this demand is not always expressed through public advertisements or tenders.** In many cases, officers and departments have internal goals to meet — but lack proactive vendors or partners who understand their constraints and can offer nimble, aligned solutions.

What Makes Government Demand Unique:

- It's **mission-driven,** not market-driven
- Funds often have **tight deadlines for utilization** (use it or lose it)
- There's immense **pressure to show outcomes,** not just activities

This leads to a situation where officials are actively looking for dependable, strategic partners who can deliver without complications, delays, or non-compliance.

2. The Lifecycle of Government Planning

To truly see hidden demand, you must learn to "read" the government from the inside out.

A. The Budgeting Phase

- Union Budget, State Budgets, and Departmental Plans are passed annually.
- Each department gets funds allocated for schemes (such as Jal Jeevan Mission, PM Gati Shakti, Ayushman Bharat, PM Kaushal Vikas Yojana, etc.)
- Within departments, district-level or block-level implementation units receive targeted budgets

B. Execution Pressure Builds

- ➢ Bureaucrats are expected to meet targets, conduct workshops, achieve enrollments, deploy tech, create awareness, and more
- ➢ Each month, quarterly, and annual reviews are conducted, and non-performing districts/departments are flagged

C. The Procurement Gap Emerges

- ➢ Most officers don't have the time or staff to float new tenders every time they face a gap
- ➢ They often reach out to:
  - Pre-empanelled vendors
  - CSR partners
  - Experts with successful pilots in other districts

Understanding this **planning-to-pressure-to-gap flow** allows you to be in the right place at the right time, without ever chasing tenders.

3. Types of Hidden Demand

A. Urgent, Unplanned Requirements

- ➢ A district needs an awareness campaign for menstrual hygiene before a minister's visit; no time for tenders
- ➢ An IT system crashes before the data submission deadline, vendor is needed urgently

B. Pilot Projects for Evaluation

- ➢ Before scaling an idea statewide, departments look for partners to test it locally
- ➢ If you can present a pilot model, budget-neutral or co-funded, you win trust

C. Mandated Initiatives without Roadmaps

- Officers are told to train 5,000 youth, but have no training partner yet
- Anganwadi workers must be trained in mental health awareness, but the curriculum is missing

These are the moments where **strategy beats speed, and credibility beats connections.**

D. Informal But Recurring Needs

- Designing banners, printing brochures, managing transport for VIP events, and maintaining district websites
- These are done without fresh tenders, only if someone dependable is already in touch

E. CSR & Public-Private Partnerships (PPP)

- Collaborating with PSUs under CSR for infrastructure, training, skilling, and education
- Departments welcome partners that reduce their budget load but help achieve mission targets

4. Where to Spot This Demand

A. Go Beyond Tender Portals

- Tender portals only show **public demand**
- Most hidden demand lives in **file notes, meetings, WhatsApp groups, and officer discussions**

B. Read Departmental Reports

- Annual Reports, Evaluation Documents, and Impact Assessments clearly show gaps and bottlenecks

C. Monitor State & District Plans

- Every state's Planning Department and Niti Aayog-aligned portals show objectives
- The District Collector's Office often publishes progress reports with performance indicators

D. Use Strategic RTI

- File RTIs asking for vendors used in a department for the last 2 years
- Spot non-tendered categories, repeat vendor names, and seasonal patterns

E. Track Officer Transfers

- When an officer who liked your work gets transferred, they may invite you again to their new department
- Maintain relations through LinkedIn, formal email updates

5. Aligning Your Business with Hidden Demand

It's not enough to spot demand. You must shape your offering to meet it.

A. Translate Your Offer into Government-Speak

Instead of saying "We do digital marketing," say:

"We support citizen engagement campaigns under flagship missions by designing IEC (Information, Education, Communication) and digital outreach plans aligned with state objectives."

B. Create Modular Proposals

- Show a ₹5 Lakh version, ₹25 Lakh version, and ₹1 Cr version of your offering
- Officers like flexibility and scalability

C. Offer Measurable KPIs

- Impact = more than delivery
- Suggest how your service will improve outcomes (e.g., increase enrolment, reduce dropout, improve health metrics)

D. Present Success Stories

- Share case studies with proof, before-and-after pictures, testimonials, and data comparisons

E. Conduct Awareness Sessions

- Offer to do one free seminar/webinar on a mission-aligned topic, position yourself as a domain expert, not a vendor

From Supplier to Strategic Partner

This transformation happens when:

- You help **plan the solution,** not just deliver
- You provide **feedback and real-time insights** to officers
- You suggest how your model could **save costs, increase speed, or build capacity**

Officers begin to loop you into planning meetings, even for unrelated departments. Your visibility multiplies. You're now seen as **"the go-to guy".**

Real Entrepreneurs Winning with Hidden Demand

Case Study 1: Nutrition Awareness Agency

A small startup offered free training sessions on child nutrition in tribal districts. Their initiative got featured in the state newspaper and was picked up by the Women and Child Development Department for a state-wide scale-up.

Case Study 2: Drone Company in Agriculture

Instead of selling drones, this firm offered "Smart Krishi Mapping Pilots" in 3 blocks. The Agriculture Department used the data in presentations to Delhi, and the company got empanelled without bidding.

Case Study 3: Skilling Startup

A soft-skills training company did workshops for 100 unemployed youth in one district under Skill India. Their post-program employment data was so impressive, they were included in the state RFP as a suggested vendor.

Mindset: See Gaps as Gold

Most entrepreneurs look at government demand like this:

"Tell me what you need, and I'll quote."

Strategic entrepreneurs look like this:

"Here's a gap in your scheme. I have a way to fix it faster and cheaper. Want to try a pilot?"

They understand:

- Not every opportunity is listed
- Not every rupee is spent

- Not every officer wants excuses; they want execution

If you solve that pain, you become irreplaceable.

Don't Just Wait. Walk In.

Hidden demand in the government is like submerged icebergs; the real mass lies beneath the surface. The smart businesses aren't floating above. They're diving in.

If you:

- Understand the pressure points of departments
- Speak their language
- Offer measurable, policy-aligned outcomes
- Build ethical relationships

...then your **business will win again and again,** without needing to bid, beg, or borrow influence.

You're no longer playing the game others are stuck in. You're playing the **strategy game.**

In the next chapter, we'll guide you to build your own Strategic Government Offer, a ready-to-present solution that aligns with real demand and makes you stand out instantly.

Chapter 3

BUILDING YOUR STRATEGIC GOVERNMENT OFFER

Why Do You Need a Strategic Government Offer

A strategic government offer is not just a service brochure. It is a carefully positioned, policy-aligned, **need-sensitive solution that makes officers say, "This is exactly what we need."**

In this chapter, we will walk you through:

- How to shape your offer so it aligns with government missions
- Frameworks to position your service or product strategically
- Templates and language that work inside the system
- Real-life examples of winning offers
- Methods to pre-position yourself even before presenting your offer
- How to make your offer scalable, sustainable, and auditable
- Building a Value Stack that sells itself

What Is a Strategic Government Offer?

A Strategic Government Offer (SGO) is a custom-built solution tailored to:

- Match policy goals
- Solve immediate departmental problems
- Fit budget realities and utilization cycles
- Be deployable quickly

Think of it as a mini-proposal that speaks the officer's language and solves their pain.

This is not a brochure.

This is a strategy tool.

It shows you understand their scheme, their struggle, and their stakeholders.

Components of an SGO:

- Mission-aligned title
- Problem-solution clarity
- Measurable outcomes
- Process map or execution flow
- Budget adaptability
- Compliance-safe delivery model
- Risk coverage or mitigation plan
- Monitoring & evaluation logic

Aligning With Government Missions

Every scheme or project launched by the government is rooted in a national or state mission. These are vision-driven umbrellas, and departments work as implementation arms.

Your offer must mirror these visions. That's how it gets relevance.

Example: Don't Say This:

"We provide digital literacy workshops."

Say This Instead:

"We contribute to Digital India by offering scalable digital literacy bootcamps to underserved rural students using vernacular e-learning modules."

Strategic Positioning Angle:

- Find the policy context in government documents
- Pick the language used in that scheme
- Reflect those words in your offer headline
- Highlight how you will support the target outcomes mentioned in the scheme guidelines

Shown below is a done-for-you framework for certain Government departments/missions; similarly, you can map out for areas that are relevant to you.

A Framework for Mapping

Government Mission	Related Department	Key Objectives	Offer Connection
Jal Jeevan Mission	Rural Development	Water Quality, Household Taps	IoT Water Monitoring System
PM Gati Shakti	Urban Local Bodies	Infrastructure Planning	GIS Mapping Tools for Traffic
Swachh Bharat	Urban Affairs, Health	Cleanliness Index	Waste Management Training

Startup India	MSME, DPIIT	Entrepreneurship	Rural Incubation Labs

Understanding the Officer's Pain-Points & Pressure

Most proposals fail because they are company-centric. Officers care about their deliverables, not your product.

Officers face:

- **Limited time:** Tight fund utilization windows
- **Audit pressure:** Everything needs documentation
- **Political visibility:** Ministers ask for results
- **Public scrutiny:** Media and RTI impact
- **HR gaps:** Too few staff to execute many tasks

Your offer must say: **"We reduce your load. We get your results. We don't increase your risk."**

Here is a Format to Use:

"Under [Scheme], multiple [blocks/wards] are lacking [service]. Our model solves it by [action], within [timeframe], monitored through [method]. We support department staff with trained resources."

Example:

> "Under PMKVY, the tribal areas of Chhattisgarh lack vocational skill centers. Our 30-day 'mobile skilling labs' train youth using certified trainers, monitored via Geo-tagged attendance and video proof."

The Format of a Winning Strategic Government Offer

A. Title:

"Mobile Solar Labs for Last-Mile Skill Training under Skill India Mission"

B. Summary:

This offer provides an end-to-end skill deployment model via solar-powered mobile training labs, especially designed for geographies with no existing infrastructure.

C. Relevance:

Direct alignment with Skill India, Tribal Welfare Mission, and Green Energy Adoption

D. Objectives:

- Train 1,500 tribal youth in solar and battery installation
- Create 100+ micro-entrepreneurs within 60 days post-training
- Reduce dropout rate using gamified learning

E. Delivery:

- 5 Mobile Vans fitted with tools and AV setup
- SHG network for mobilisation
- NSDC-certified trainers
- Livelihood tie-ups with solar startups

F. Budget Options:

- ₹10L (2 Vans for 1 district)
- ₹20L (5 Vans full district pilot)
- ₹50L (2 District Cluster Model)

G. Monitoring Plan:

- GPS tracking of vans
- Skill pre-post test forms
- Real-time dashboard for officers

Strategic Offers That Worked: Some Case Studies

These real-world cases show how small firms cracked large government doors.

Case Study 1: Affordable Eye Care That Scaled 4 Districts

A 2-member optometry firm created a mobile eye care bus that served 6 schools in Rajasthan.

- The project was pitched as part of Beti Bachao - Girl Child Health Checkup.
- The District Collector got CSR support to fund it.
- Now it's scaled to 4 districts.

Case Study 2: Drone-Based Soil Health Mapping

An Agri-tech founder designed a pilot project for drone-based soil testing. Framed under the Doubling Farmers' Income mission, it was picked by the Horticulture Department as a pilot for subsidy design.

Case Study 3: Panchayat Kiosk Kit

A tech startup designed a plug-and-play kiosk for Gram Panchayats to apply digitally for schemes. It was positioned under Digital India, funded via the district innovation challenge funds.

Strategic Tools to Elevate Your Offer

A. Policy Scan Toolkit:

Before writing, research:

- Ministerial Budget Allocations
- Annual Performance Reports
- National Mission Dashboards
- CSR Activity Reports of PSUs in the Target District

B. Offer Visualiser Toolkit:

Your 3-page offer should include:

- Mind Map of the Model
- Before/After Process Infographic
- Table of Deliverables vs Time

C. Scalability Framework:

Plan offers in tiers:

- **Pilot Tier:** ₹3-5 Lakhs, 1 block, proof of concept
- **Expansion Tier:** ₹10-15 Lakhs, district level
- **Flagship Tier:** ₹50+ Lakhs, cross-district scale

Each tier should list unique KPIs and scale mechanics.

D. Value Stack Blueprint:

Every offer must have a "value beyond money" story:

- What stress does it reduce for the officer?
- What media/social visibility can the department get?
- What future-ready system does it initiate?

Common Mistakes That Cost You Everything

- **Treating Government Like B2B:** It's not B2B, it's B2G (Business to Government). Procurement is emotional + political + compliant.
- **No Context:** Offers not rooted in mission guidelines = instant rejection.
- **Being Generic:** Every district has different problems. Generic offers = disrespect.
- **Budget Misfit:** Offering a ₹1Cr model to a department with ₹10L IEC (Information, Education, Communication) fund.
- **Not Offering Pilot:** Without proof-of-concept, few officers risk your new model.

Offering a Presentation That Opens Doors

Once your offer is ready, here is your:

Step-by-Step Rollout Plan:

1. **Refine it to 2 formats:**
    - Short WhatsApp Summary (Title + Impact + Ask)
    - Detailed 2-Pager with Visuals
2. **Share with the relevant officer** via WhatsApp and official email
3. **Wait 48 hours,** then call the PA/Officer and request a 5-minute briefing
4. **Prepare a one-slide explainer** for Zoom or a physical meeting
5. **Leave behind** a printed version with your photo/business card

A Bonus Tip

Always carry a **'Results Booklet':** images, media coverage, testimonials, dashboards from past work.

It builds instant trust.

Offer Like a Strategic Ally, Not a Vendor

Your goal is not just to "get work." Your goal is to become the go-to partner for meaningful government initiatives.

In this game:

- The best offer wins, not the cheapest quote.
- Strategy beats shouting.
- Alignment beats networking.

So build your Strategic Government Offer like your ticket to the transformation table.

In the next chapter, we'll go deep into how to build your Visibility & Access so that your name travels further than your proposal, and officials start calling you.

Chapter 4

VISIBILITY AND ACCESS: BECOMING KNOWN BEFORE YOU'RE NEEDED

Strategy Alone Isn't Enough

"You can have the most policy-aligned, brilliantly crafted government offer in the world, but if no one in the system knows you exist, your chances are slim."

In government business, **visibility precedes viability.**

This chapter is your roadmap to becoming visible, credible, and accessible to decision-makers before they have a need, so that when they do, they think of you.

Why Visibility Matters More Than Ever

Unlike private markets, the government is not scanning Instagram for vendors.

It is governed by:

- **Hierarchy:** A known name moves faster through channels
- **Perception:** Officers judge your risk factor by your credibility
- **Memory:** Your name must be easy to recall when decisions are made

Being visible isn't about advertising. It's about relevance, recall, and respect.

Types of Visibility that Matter in Government

A. Strategic Visibility

You become known as a **go-to name** in a specific domain (e.g., Water Management in Rajasthan).

B. Localised Visibility

Your name travels within **district-level** systems, between Collectors, CDOs, and DMs.

C. Mission-Centric Visibility

You are associated with a **National/State Scheme** (e.g., Digital India, PM-KUSUM).

D. Technical Visibility

Your work is referred to in reports, papers, conferences, or reviewed by technical committees.

E. Social-Impact Visibility

You create buzz with outcomes showcased in **CSR reports,** media stories, and public events.

The Visibility Funnel

You need a structured plan to go from Unknown to Trusted.

Phase 1: Introduce

- Identify 10 relevant officers per department
- Use WhatsApp messages, emails, and social media posts

- Send your strategic offer as a WhatsApp-ready summary (Title + Outcome + Ask)

Phase 2: Engage

- Attend public consultations or local seminars
- Ask relevant questions during webinars
- Send impact stories via WhatsApp every 2 weeks

Phase 3: Reinforce

- Share updates, dashboards, and media coverage
- Tag relevant officials in scheme-aligned LinkedIn posts
- Celebrate government success stories (not just your own)

Phase 4: Become Familiar

- Officers begin to recognise your face, name, and tone
- They forward your offers internally or to peers
- Some initiate conversation with you, that's the shift

Access: The Art of Ethical Reach

You don't need to "push your way in." You need to design ethical access points that are:

- Low resistance
- High value
- Relationship-building, not transactional

A. Educational Entry Points

- Offer to train district staff on a specific tech or framework
- Present knowledge sessions aligned with scheme objectives
- Write a 2-page explainer on a burning problem with solutions and outcomes

B. Network Entry Points

- Connect with government vendors, trainers, or NGOs already inside the system
- Volunteer on joint initiatives (awareness drives, health camps, digital days)
- Offer **free pilots** or proof-of-concept during the scheme launch week

C. Media Access Points

- Share stories with local journalists covering district administration
- Co-brand impact work with local influencers, SHG leaders, or teachers

D. Institutional Entry Points

- Join working groups, state innovation challenges, and Smart City meetups
- Apply for pilot innovation grants via Atal Incubation Centres or state startup missions

Building a Publicly Visible Portfolio

Officers don't trust brochures. They trust evidence.

Create an online and offline trail of your government-aligned work:

- **Case Study Deck:** PDF with Title, Pain Point, Action, Outcome, Media, Next Step
- **LinkedIn Thought Posts:** Show insights around scheme objectives and execution ideas
- **Photo Evidence:** Before-and-after visuals, Geo-tags, group photos with department staff

- **Newspaper Clippings:** Get 1 district story published, even if hyperlocal
- **WhatsApp Status:** Officers often check your DP/status. Use it to showcase recent work or headlines.

The Trust Ladder

You don't become a partner in one meeting. You ascend the ladder step by step:

Stage	Identity in an Officer's Mind	Action You Take
Stranger	Unknown	WhatsApp your offer summary
Familiar	Recalled Name	Share the past result dashboard
Reliable	One who Delivers	Show proof in the new geography
Trusted	Partner for Mission	Joint planning discussions

Keep climbing by:

- Delivering as promised
- Updating them with progress proactively
- Inviting them to events
- Sending handwritten thanks or impact notes

Mistakes That Kill Your Access

- **Too Pushy:** Repeated calls and emails without response irritate officers
- **Too Vague:** Saying "we do everything" makes you irrelevant
- **Too Selfish:** Only showcasing your product, not the public good

- **Too Political:** Using names of MLAs/Ministers for pressure backfires

Visibility Wins: Real Examples

1. The Skill Van Man

A startup founder named his project "Skill Van Man."

- His offer visuals and status updates showed live training across villages.
- Soon, DM offices began calling him for district-level deployment.

2. The Google Map Champion

An NGO mapping broken borewells in Jharkhand shared a public Google Map link with district heads.

It went viral within the Jal Shakti mission, and they were offered state-level projects.

3. The LinkedIn Influencer

A young founder wrote weekly posts connecting government missions with real field stories.

After 2 months, the Smart City CEO messaged them directly to discuss a partnership.

Your Weekly Visibility Routine

- **Monday:** Identify 2 officers and share a new insight or update
- **Wednesday:** Publish a LinkedIn post around a scheme challenge
- **Friday:** Update your WhatsApp status with an impact proof or a quote

- **Monthly:** Email your 2-pager offer to at least 5 district officers

Over 90 days, this builds cumulative recall. Consistency wins.

Make Them Remember You Before They Need You

Visibility is not vanity. In government business, it is a strategic asset.

Your name must:

- Show up where schemes are discussed
- Be whispered in rooms you're not in
- Be tied to outcomes, not noise

You don't need to be famous. You need to be visible to the right people at the right level with the right message.

And when your offer arrives, they will say: **"We've heard of you. Let's talk."**

In the next chapter, we'll decode the inner workings of government mindsets and departmental flows, so you can move like water through a maze, with clarity and purpose.

Chapter 5

UNDERSTANDING THE GOVERNMENT MINDSET AND STRUCTURE

The Government Is Not a Company

To navigate government systems, you must shed your corporate instincts.

The government is not a monolith or a single company. It's a layered, hierarchical, and protocol-driven structure where decisions are governed not by market dynamics but by **public accountability, procedural compliance,** and **policy mandates.**

This chapter is your GPS for decoding how the government thinks, acts, and decides, so your strategy isn't just smart but system-compatible.

The DNA of Indian Government Departments

A. Mission Over Metrics

Private businesses track KPIs and ROIs. Government departments track **schemes, mandates, coverage, and inclusion.** Their North Star is not profit but **public welfare and political alignment.**

B. Hierarchical Decision Making

- Decision-making flows top-down
- Communication flows bottom-up
- Everything is documented, noted, and verified

A District Magistrate might support you, but unless the **line department agrees,** the file won't move. Know the flow.

C. Risk Aversion Culture

- Government officers are trained to avoid failure
- They prefer proven, safe, known vendors or ideas
- Bold innovation scares many unless backed by higher orders

D. Reputation Management

Every officer wants to leave a legacy or at least **avoid bad press.** Your offer must be positioned as something that safeguards their image, not risks it.

Departmental Structures That Matter for You

A. Central vs State vs District

- **The Central Government** frames the policies, schemes, and funds (PMAY, PMKVY, Jal Jeevan Mission)
- **State Governments** adapt these to local realities and release budgets
- **District Administration** executes these with available resources

You must align your offer to match the execution level you want to influence.

B. Key Decision Nodes

Level	Roles to Know	Why They Matter
Centre	Joint Secretary, Director	Policy design, budget allocation
State	Commissioner, Mission Director	Scheme adaptation, RFP release
District	DM, CDO, SDM, Line Dept Heads	Execution, pilot permission

C. Line Departments

Each scheme runs under a "line department" like:

- Health
- Women & Child Development
- Rural Development
- Education
- Skill Development
- Urban Local Bodies

Each has its own file structure, officer ladder, and technical approval cycle.

File Movement and Decision Trees

To get approval, your offer must pass through:

- **Initiation:** The Line officer prepares a note
- **Recommendation:** Head of Dept gives go-ahead
- **Legal/Finance Vetting:** Ensures compliance
- **Final Sanction:** Collector/Commissioner signs off

A brilliant idea alone isn't enough. You need:

- A Note for Approval (NFA)
- A Concept Proposal
- Budget Alignment
- Past Proof of Success

Language of the Bureaucracy

The government doesn't speak in brand language.

It speaks:

- In abbreviations (NULM (National Urban Livelihoods Mission), PM-FME, SMAM)
- In keywords like: "coverage," "saturation," "convergence," "community mobilization"
- In files, not chats

Learn to write like a section officer. That earns you respect.

Example Translation:

Instead of: "We run a skilling centre for rural youth."

Say: "We facilitate convergence under DAY-NULM with domain-trained mobilizers and sector-specific instructors."

How Officers Think and Act

A. Officers Have Intent, But No Time

Most officers have:

- 10+ meetings per day
- Dozens of WhatsApp groups
- Pressure from political, audit, public, and judicial corners

So your pitch must be:

- 2 pages max
- Visually digestible
- Outcome-oriented

B. Officers Are Rotated

A Collector today might be transferred in 6 months. You need system-level buy-in, not individual loyalty. Your data, reports, and pilots must live in the file system, not just the officer's mind.

C. Officers Prefer Risk-Sharing

You must show:

- How you will co-own outcomes
- How you'll work with their existing teams
- How your model will NOT drain their bandwidth

The Power of Government Language

Speak the way they do:

- Refer to current missions and SDG alignment
- Use District Annual Plans and State Guidelines in your framing
- Present work as "Supporting the department" instead of "Solving the problem"

Use phrases like:

- "Convergence with departmental mandate"
- "Replicable in similar socio-economic blocks"
- "No additional manpower burden"
- "Digitally traceable model"

How to Read Government Signals

A. Reading Circulars

Every circular is a clue:

- Problem area
- Preferred delivery approach
- Budget ceiling
- Reporting format

Learn to decode circulars to identify:

- Entry points
- Partner expectations
- Deadlines

B. Watching Scheme Flow

Track:

- Portal announcements
- Last year's unutilized budgets
- Who the current vendors are

C. Following Tender vs Non-Tender Routes

Not everything is a tender. Many innovations enter through:

- Pilot programs
- NGO tie-ups
- Special Task Forces
- CSR integrations

Working with Departments: Real Strategies

Action	Department Response
Offer a free pilot	Low-risk curiosity
Share media coverage	Trust amplification
Send a monthly field report	Institutional memory build-up
Offer dashboard access	Real-time monitoring aid
Write policy brief	Strategic value alignment

Avoiding Red Flags

Never:

- Claim support without a formal letter
- Push beyond protocol (e.g., skipping levels)
- Present overly commercial models
- Use political pressure
- Miss review meetings

Always:

- Confirm alignment with the scheme
- Clarify that you don't require a budget immediately
- Offer co-created implementation

Winning the Officer's Mind

You win when the officer says:

"This helps me do my job better without extra work or compliance risk."

Your model should:

- Help them meet KPIs
- Simplify their reports
- Avoid media backlash
- Make them look proactive

Move Like Water, Not Like a Hammer

You don't push your way in. You shape your offering to fit the **containers of governance.**

Once you know how officers think, what departments value, and how systems move, your strategy will no longer be friction-based. It will be flow-based.

In the next chapter, we'll explore how to create proof-of-concept and strategic pilots that inspire officers to say, "Let's replicate this."

Chapter 6

Designing Pilot Projects That Prove and Persuade

Why Pilots Are the Bridge Between Idea and Implementation

In government, scepticism is the default setting. Officers are flooded with promises, proposals, and vendors every day. What cuts through the noise is a pilot project that demonstrates real impact, alignment, and feasibility.

A pilot project allows you to say, "We've done it before, at no cost to you, and here's the proof."

This is the difference between theory and trust. In this chapter, we explore how to design, deploy, and document pilots that open doors to large-scale implementation.

What Makes a Pilot Project Powerful

A. Minimal Risk for Government

Your pilot should require:

- No budget from the department
- No major policy shift
- No extra manpower

B. High Visibility for Impact

Ensure:

- Field-based results in 30–60 days
- Involvement of existing govt staff
- Beneficiaries or public feedback built in

C. Easy to Explain Upward

Officers should be able to present your pilot to seniors in a simple note:

"This model was tested in the XYZ block. Cost-neutral. Community-led. Scalable."

D. Designed to Integrate

Your pilot should use:

- Existing government data
- Department's reporting tools
- Scheme-aligned objectives

E. Emotionally Resonant Outcomes

Government officials respond strongly to public-facing wins:

- Community appreciation events
- Testimonies of beneficiaries
- Social media and local media coverage

A pilot that triggers goodwill in the field often finds traction in the hierarchy.

Types of Pilot Projects That Work

A. Short-Term Skill Camps

- Conduct a 7-day training with placement tie-ups under a skill scheme
- Show mobilization, attendance, and outcome

B. Mobile Service Vans

- Health checkups, documentation services, and awareness
- Can cover 5–10 villages in a week

C. Tech-Based Monitoring Dashboards

- Offer dashboards using the government's own MIS data
- Visual, filterable, role-based access

D. Demonstration Farms or Sites

- In agriculture, sanitation, and housing
- Show proof of concept physically

E. Co-Branded Public Events

- CSR-day, women empowerment week, skill fairs
- Showcase your presence with media/photo coverage

F. Behaviour Change Campaigns

- Run community engagement and IEC pilots on cleanliness, nutrition, and digital access
- Show measurable change in awareness, practice, or attendance

G. Advisory or Consulting Pilots

- Frame a small research or data-collection-based model for decision support

- Useful in urban local bodies, planning departments, or innovation cells

How to Frame the Pilot

Use this template:

"We propose a 30-day pilot under [scheme] in [block] to demonstrate outcome-focused delivery using existing infrastructure and manpower. No financial ask. We will co-brand, document, and provide weekly updates."

Add details like:

- Partner NGO (if any)
- Days of operation
- Expected beneficiaries
- Contact person for coordination

Keep language humble, aligned, and cooperative. Make the officer feel like the initiator or patron of the effort.

Getting Approvals Without Bureaucracy

- Prepare a Pilot Proposal (max 4 pages)
- Include a one-page flyer/briefing note for WhatsApp circulation
- Attach any previous case studies or partner letters
- Send it via email AND submit a hard copy
- Don't wait for formal sanction. Begin with a district-level consent and intent letter or verbal nod

Follow up consistently, and ensure:

- PA knows your face

- You build goodwill with the clerk handling files
- You respect protocol and hierarchy

Executing the Pilot Like a Pro

A. Ground Team

- Use trained local volunteers
- Engage anganwadi workers, SHGs, and Panchayat bodies
- Daily monitoring using WhatsApp groups

B. Officer Involvement

- Include them in Day 1 and Day Last
- Offer them to inaugurate or felicitate beneficiaries
- Invite media and give the officer proper credit

C. Documentation

- Daily photos geo-tagged
- Attendance sheets, activity logs
- Beneficiary ID + Testimony + Outcome

D. Media Coverage

- Send daily update to local journalist WhatsApp groups
- Tag department handles or officers (if comfortable)
- Push visual storytelling

E. Digital Reporting

- Use Google Forms for team updates
- Real-time dashboards via Google Sheets or simple apps
- Create a link that can be shared up the ladder

What to Do After the Pilot Ends

- Prepare a **Pilot Outcome Report**
    - **Include:** Objectives, Methodology, Results, Visuals, Lessons, Replication Model
    - **Keep it short and attractive:** 6 pages with photos, quotes, metrics
- Submit a **Follow-Up Proposal**
    - **Offer:** Scaling plan, Cost per unit, Roles required, State-wide replication estimate

"Here's how we can replicate this across 15 blocks, within existing budget and teams."

- Pitch a Review Meeting Presentation
- Ask the officer for 5 minutes to present at the monthly meetings
- Show success, offer roadmap, take questions

From Pilot to Policy: How Pilots Win Endorsements

Well-designed pilots often:

- Get featured in State Review Meetings
- Are discussed in video conferences with Ministries
- Attract CSR partners or donor funding
- Are converted into State-wide programs

Ensure you:

- Keep the officer in the loop post-pilot
- Acknowledge his/her support publicly

- Deliver the final report personally
- Present the scalability model in terms of cost, team, infrastructure, and ROI for the government

Red Flags to Avoid

- Over-promising impact or scale
- Starting without district consent
- Poor daily communication
- Weak documentation and reporting
- Treating it like a PR activity without field substance
- Relying only on one officer for support

Always align with:

- Scheme goals
- District priorities
- Officer comfort levels
- Timing (avoid election periods, audits, transfers)

Real Pilot Examples (Templates)

Sector	Pilot Idea	Result
Education	Digital smart class with local teachers	Adopted in 3 blocks
Sanitation	Model toilet with community mason	Endorsed by Gram Sabha
Skilling	10-day women's tailoring camp	40% got orders post-camp
Governance	RTI tracking dashboard for the district	DM cited in the review meeting

Agriculture	Bio-input demo plots for yield improvement	Funded by the state's agri dept
Health	Anaemia testing + nutrition awareness	School-based pilot scaled by NHM

Pilots Are Your Gateway

A pilot is your **proof of seriousness,** your **trial run,** and your **entry pass.**

If your offer is your resume, the pilot is your internship.

Do it well, and the government will ask you to stay and scale.

Success comes not to those who pitch perfectly, but to those who perform tangibly.

In the next chapter, we'll cover how to turn these pilots into **institutional partnerships** that last for years.

Chapter 7

FROM PILOT TO PARTNERSHIP

Creating Long-Term Institutional Relationships

Why Partnerships Matter More Than Projects

After a successful pilot, many businesses make the mistake of sitting back, waiting for the government to call them. But in the world of strategic government consulting, **a pilot is not the end;** it's the beginning of a relationship. And that relationship must mature into a **structured partnership.**

In this chapter, we move beyond "project-mode thinking" and show how to institutionalize your engagement with the government through frameworks, MoUs, regular reviews, and embedded collaborations, all without the need for tenders or permanent contracts.

What Is an Institutional Partnership?

An institutional partnership is not a one-time assignment. It's a formal or informal collaboration where your business becomes a trusted solution provider to a department, scheme, or government function.

Think of it like this:

- A vendor solves a problem once.
- A partner becomes part of the solution ecosystem.

Institutional partnerships lead to:

- Repeated projects without retendering
- Being called into strategy meetings
- Getting credit in departmental reviews
- ●Long-term visibility with decision-makers

Modes of Partnership That Work

Let's explore common forms of partnerships that Indian government departments already recognize:

A. MoU-Based Association

- Signed at the district or state level
- Lists the scope of work, roles, and non-financial commitments
- Often with CSR arms, NGOs, or startups

B. Advisory/Expert Panel Inclusion

- You are inducted as a non-paid expert or advisor
- Get access to data, plans, and meetings
- Influence design and implementation

C. Nodal or Anchor Partner for a Theme

- For example: digital literacy, menstrual hygiene, drone usage
- The officer mentions your name in the state reviews

D. Resource Person Status

- You are invited to train or guide staff
- Gets you a seat at all district or state events

E. Embedded Model

- Your team is placed within govt offices for support
- Works for tech models, monitoring cells, and field training teams

F. Innovation Cell Association

- You're registered with the district or ministry innovation cells
- They push your idea across geographies

These are **tender-free,** trust-based, and **scalable.**

Building A Case for The Partnership

The biggest mistake is asking for a partnership. The right approach is to **build a strong case** for why your inclusion helps the department.

Your pitch must answer these:

- What are we solving?
- How do we fit into existing schemes?
- What do we commit (non-financial)?
- What visibility, monitoring, and outcomes can we offer?
- How will this free up department bandwidth?

Your previous pilot report is your passport here.

Frame your proposal as:

"We propose a deeper integration under [mission/scheme] as a knowledge or execution partner. No cost to the department. We commit dedicated manpower, daily reporting, capacity-building, and handholding. Outcomes tracked monthly. Here's what we've already achieved."

Identifying the Right Level of Partnership

Different Types of Partnerships that Work at Different Levels

Level	Type of Partnership	Ideal For
Block	Anchor Partner for Field Activity	Skill camps, awareness drives
District	MoU for Execution Support	IEC, health, education, SHG
Division	Innovation Cell Empanelment	Agri-tech, EdTech
State	Nodal Agency Collaboration	CSR, IT, dashboards
Ministry	Expert Panel or Advisory Role	National scaling, data analysis

Start where you're respected, and scale where you're noticed.

How to Formalize the Relationship

Here's how to structure your move from pilot to partner:

A. Draft a Concept Note

- **Title:** Strategic Partnership for [Theme/Sector]
- **Context:** Based on a successful pilot in [location]
- **Objectives:** Better outcomes, faster execution, field feedback loop
- **Scope:** What you'll do and what you'll not
- **Duration:** 6–12 months
- **Monitoring:** Weekly dashboard, Monthly review
- **Contact:** 1 Nodal officer + 1 Liaison person from your side

B. Request a Meeting With Department Head

- Present printed proposal + one-page brief
- Bring visuals: dashboard, media, feedback letters
- Offer no financial ask, only outcome delivery

C. Submit Follow-Up Communication

- Email with subject: "Follow-up: Strategic Partnership on [X] – as discussed"
- Attach final PDF + any field documentation.

D. Ask for a Working-Level Go-Ahead

- Even without an MoU, get written consent from the nodal officer
- Keep internal WhatsApp/Slack for updates

E. Build a Backwards-Compatible Team

- Hire or partner with local coordinators
- Use youth, volunteers, SHGs
- Assign one government nodal contact

Becoming Invaluable to the Government

Government officers **don't partner with brands; they partner with people they trust.**

You must become someone they see as:

- Responsive
- Respectful of hierarchy
- Effective with minimal supervision
- Aligned with larger departmental goals
- Discreet and ethical

Build trust by:

- Being available without being clingy
- Communicating field updates proactively
- Not showing off without permission
- Giving officers public credit in media or presentations
- Understanding their pressure points and timelines

You're not just a business partner; you're a bandwidth saver.

Sustaining and Scaling the Partnership

Once the partnership is in place:

A. Institutionalize Monthly Reviews

- Use Google Meet, review decks, and field data
- Ask the department to assign a single nodal person

B. Offer Training and Capacity Building

- For district staff, SHGs, and Panchayat
- Create easy-to-use manuals and videos
- Organize refresher camps or TOTs (Training of Trainers)

C. Expand Geographically

- Propose: "We've done this in 2 blocks. Let's try 4 more."
- Scale with the same manpower but new district officials
- Build local champions

D. Create Sustainability Model

- Map out how the government can continue without you
- Document SOPs, toolkit, or handbooks
- Train the internal team so your exit looks graceful

Real Examples of Institutional Partnerships

Partner	Department	Nature of Partnership	Outcome
Startup: AgriAI	Department of Agriculture, Punjab	Dashboard + Demo Plots	Now State PMU Partner
NGO: Vikas Foundation	Women & Child, Odisha	Training of Trainers + IEC	MoU for 3 years
CSR Arm: Bharat CSR	Education, MP	Smart Class Kits + App	Mentioned in 2 State Reviews
Tech: HealthX	NHM, Chhattisgarh	Anaemia Dashboard	Added to Health Cell permanently

Common Pitfalls to Avoid

- Being too eager to push the partnership paperwork too early
- Asking for money in the first engagement
- Acting entitled because your pilot succeeded
- Not documenting your efforts consistently
- Leaving field teams unmonitored
- Not understanding political timing (elections, transfers, code of conduct)
- Speaking ill of other vendors or officers

Partnership is a Process, Not a Proposal

You don't "get" a partnership, you earn it.

You earn it by showing up, solving problems, communicating

clearly, and respecting systems. You become part of the government's extended ecosystem, someone they rely on when real change is needed.

You don't fight for space. You **grow into the space** by being helpful, consistent, and humble.

Becoming the Government's Go-To Partner

- Start with a successful pilot
- Identify natural areas for collaboration
- Frame value-first partnership proposals
- Build trust through consistent field delivery
- Create scale-ready and exit-friendly models
- Get included in official meetings, reviews, and committees
- Become a long-term insider without losing your **outside expertise**

In the next chapter, we'll explore how to scale your efforts beyond one region and take your strategy to the state and national level.

Chapter 8

Scaling Your Government Strategy to the State and National Level

Once you have created a local success story and turned a pilot into a partnership, the real opportunity opens up: **taking your model statewide or even nationally.** This is where your strategy can evolve from impact to influence, from presence to policy relevance.

But scaling government engagement is not just about sending the same proposal to higher offices. It requires new thinking, new allies, and stronger systems. Here, we show you how to plan, position, and pitch for replication at scale.

Leverage State Innovation Units and Startup Cells

Most Indian states now have innovation cells or startup missions. They are actively looking for scalable, high-impact models that solve public problems. Align your work with their objectives and become part of the ecosystem.

Benefits include:

- Direct access to decision-makers
- Faster vetting process
- Public endorsements and showcases
- Entry into multiple departments through one window

Be sure to document your outcomes with state-specific relevance. Tailor your pitch deck to regional pain points.

Engage Policy Influencers and Development Think Tanks

To get national traction, you must be visible in the intellectual policy space.

Engage with:

- NITI Aayog officials
- Development Alternatives, CEEW, PRS Legislative
- State Development Commissions

How?

- Attend and speak at policy hackathons, summits
- Publish op-eds and articles showcasing outcomes
- Co-create white papers with these institutions

These relationships open doors to policymakers who drive the big moves.

Use Media Strategically

Your work should be in the public eye, not just social media, but sectoral and regional news:

- Publish feature stories with before-and-after case studies
- Partner with credible development journalism outlets
- Offer officers and community leaders to speak about the success

When a senior officer sees coverage of a successful model from another state, it triggers curiosity and often leads to replication.

Institutionalize Through State Circulars and GRs

A game-changing step in scale is getting your model institutionalized in an official **government circular** or **Government Resolution (GR).**

This means:

- Departments are authorized to work with you
- Field officers are directed to cooperate
- Budgetary allocations can be aligned

To make this happen:

- Draft a sample circular for the officer
- Show benefits: cost, scale, compliance
- Use language that bureaucrats resonate with: efficiency, replicability, transparency

Build Your Policy Memory

As you scale, create a live database of:

- Key decisions made
- Who supported what

- What documents helped
- What pushbacks occurred, and how they were addressed

This policy memory becomes your strategic weapon as you move into new territories and replicate more easily.

Scale with Outcome-Based Contracts

Many departments are now open to **Output or Outcome-Based Agreements.** Instead of tenders or annual contracts, they prefer models where payment is linked to impact.

Use this to your advantage:

- Create clear deliverables (X% improvement, Y no. of beneficiaries)
- Suggest third-party auditing
- Offer staggered, milestone-based implementation

Outcome-based models build trust, speed up clearance, and increase your credibility across states.

Align with Global Frameworks

If your work aligns with Sustainable Development Goals (SDGs), use that language while presenting to national bodies. Many ministries are now required to report on SDG progress.

Aligning helps:

- Tap into global grant mechanisms
- Partner with UNDP, UNICEF, WHO, etc.
- Gain preference in Smart City, AMRUT, and Swachh Bharat projects

Build a Policy-Ready Internal Team

As you scale, your internal capabilities must evolve too:

- Hire ex-bureaucrats or retired government consultants
- Train your field team on government etiquette, reporting
- Appoint a documentation head to handle case studies, dashboards, and MoUs

Policy work is slower, but deeper. Your team must adapt.

Participate in Government Challenges and Sandboxes

Many ministries now run innovation challenges or set up regulatory sandboxes.

These offer you:

- Funding
- Policy backing
- Exposure to multiple states at once

Examples:

- Ministry of Education's EdTech Challenge
- MeitY Sandbox for Digital Public Goods
- Smart City Hackathons

These create nationwide exposure and endorsements.

Codify Your Government Partnership Model

Eventually, your value lies not just in what you deliver but in how you partner.

Codify this into a handbook:

- Government Partnership SOP
- MOU samples
- Compliance framework
- Outcome measurement toolkit

Offer this to states that wish to replicate your work. When you make government collaboration easy, scale becomes inevitable.

Strategy That Scales

- Create a standard, document-backed, outcome-driven model
- Find and empower state or national-level bureaucratic champions
- Align with national missions and policy windows
- Use partnerships and coalitions to enable the spread
- Institutionalize via circulars, GRs, and formal MoUs
- Tap into SDG narratives and policy frameworks
- Build internal systems to manage the scale

Strategy isn't just about getting in. It's about getting invited back, again and again, at a higher level.

Next, we explore how to **fund your scaling journey using CSR,** multilateral grants, and ethical revenue streams.

Chapter 9

FUNDING YOUR GOVERNMENT STRATEGY: ETHICAL AND SCALABLE MODELS

Many entrepreneurs dream of scaling their government business model, but often get stuck at the question:

Where will the money come from?

The good news is that India's ecosystem is rich with funding pathways that are both ethical and strategic.

Whether you're a startup, a social enterprise, or an established SME, this chapter helps you navigate the three most viable sources of government-aligned funding: **CSR funds, multilateral agencies, and revenue-linked government payments.**

Tapping into CSR Funds

India's Companies Act mandates that firms with a certain level of profitability must spend 2% of their net profits on Corporate Social Responsibility (CSR). This pool amounts to over ₹20,000 crores annually. Much of this is underutilized.

How to Access It:

- **Identify CSR-aligned departments:** Many large corporations have CSR wings focused on education, skilling, sanitation, health, and environment.
- **Structure your offering as impact-based:** You are not just a service provider, you are a solution to a social challenge.
- **Package your project with outcomes:** Include baseline data, projected impact, and monitoring tools.
- **Use CSR portals:** Government-run portals like the MCA CSR Exchange and private ones like Goodera and CSRBox help connect you to corporate donors.

CSR allows you to do pilot or scale-up work without charging the government, yet working closely with it.

Bonus Strategy

- Offer CSR donors co-branding opportunities with local departments.
- Prepare a pitch deck showing how their brand will be seen solving real problems at the grassroots level.
- Include third-party validation metrics for credibility.

Accessing Multilateral and Bilateral Grants

Agencies like the UNDP, World Bank, Bill & Melinda Gates Foundation, and GIZ fund initiatives that align with national development priorities.

These organizations love models that:

- Work with the government
- Are scalable
- Show community impact

How to Get in:

- Register your entity on grant platforms (e.g., GrantStation, Devex, UN Global Marketplace)
- Stay alert to calls for proposals, many are cyclical (annual, bi-annual)
- Build partnerships, collaborate with NGOs or academic institutions with past track records

Bonus Tips

- Form a dedicated grant-writing team or outsource it to professionals.
- Leverage government MoUs and letters of support when applying, they drastically improve your chances.
- Frame your project in Sustainable Development Goals (SDG) language.

Monetizing Through Outcome-Based Revenue

Many Indian departments now allow **direct payment models** if your intervention leads to a measurable outcome:

Examples:

- Reduction in dropout rates
- Increase in vaccination rates
- Digital adoption in rural districts

Instead of traditional tenders, departments sign MoUs or Pay-for-Performance Contracts.

Expand It Further:

- Use blockchain or dashboards to make outcomes transparent.
- Offer a revenue-sharing model: the government saves money, and you earn for success.
- Propose hybrid projects where part of the funding is fixed, and the rest is linked to outcomes.

Crowd-Investing and Local Philanthropy

For early pilots, look close to home:

- Local industrialists or business leaders often support district-level impact
- Crowd-investment platforms now allow pooled funding for social projects (like Rang De, ImpactGuru)
- Your first ₹5-10 lakh can come from your own network when the intent and model are solid

Make It Work:

- Use storytelling: show how ₹1,000 changes a life.
- Offer updates and testimonials to backers.
- Create short documentaries post-pilot to inspire more funding.

Using Government Incubators and State Startup Missions

Many state governments run incubators and accelerators that offer funding:

- Seed grants (₹5–25 lakh)
- Monthly stipends
- Tech infrastructure and mentorship

Some examples:

- Kerala Startup Mission
- Startup Odisha
- T-Hub Telangana

Bonus Tips

- Always tailor your pitch to the **state's development vision.**
- Highlight how your solution helps the state save or earn money.
- Build relationships with the nodal officers running these incubators.

Forming Strategic Consortia

If you're not eligible for grants yourself, partner with those who are:

- NGOs with FCRA clearance
- Academic institutions with research budgets
- Startups already empaneled with state agencies

Expand the Model:

- Use your IP (intellectual property) and license it to the consortium.
- You lead the delivery; partners handle the compliance and funding.
- Document everything through clear MoUs to ensure transparency.

Building a Financial Model That Converts Impact into Revenue

Don't just seek donations or grants.

Build a financial engine that:

- Tracks units of impact (per student, per village, per officer)
- Links cost per unit to pricing models
- Builds a dashboard that shows ROI on public spending

Extend This:

- Create a SaaS-like model: monthly retainer from departments based on scale.
- Offer a toolkit to other districts/states as a white-labeled impact package.
- Maintain an impact fund within your organization to support long gestation projects.

You Don't Need to Beg for Funds. You Need to Align

- CSR funds = strategic pilot capital
- Multilateral grants = credibility and scale
- Outcome-based contracts = recurring ethical revenue
- Startup missions = early support, infrastructure

- Consortia = fast access to the ecosystem
- Crowd capital = early validation

The real capital is not just money, it's **credibility, evidence, and alignment.**

Next, we explore how to create a government relationship dashboard and ecosystem that keeps opportunities flowing in consistently.

Chapter 10

BUILDING A GOVERNMENT RELATIONSHIP DASHBOARD

If you want to win consistently with the government, you can't rely on luck or one-off conversations. You need a **relationship dashboard,** a live, evolving system that tracks who you know, what they value, and how often you engage.

In this chapter, we go beyond CRM software.

We help you build a strategic operating system to:

- Track your visibility
- Map key influencers
- Identify warm departments
- Plan engagements and follow-ups
- Benchmark outcomes
- Pre-empt risk and opportunity windows

This is the **governance layer of your government strategy.**

Step 1: Categorize Your Government Contacts

There are three categories of people you'll interact with in government:

1. **Decision-Makers:** IAS officers, department heads, principal secretaries
2. **Enablers:** Consultants, district nodal officers, sectoral experts
3. **Gatekeepers:** Clerks, personal assistants, protocol officers

You also want to note:

- Their tenure cycle: Are they stable or likely to transfer?
- Their known projects and policy interests
- Their openness to innovation (based on past pilots they've approved)

This nuanced profiling helps you customize your engagement.

Use a Sheet Like This

Name	Role	Department	Category	Interest Area	Tenure End	Last Interaction	Next Step
Mr. Sharma	DIO	NIC, Haryana	Enabler	Digital Literacy	Dec 2025	2 May 2025	Share pilot update

Step 2: Heat Map Your Influence Zones

You can't be everywhere at once. Influence heat mapping is how you focus.

Score each zone (state, department, district) across 3 dimensions:

- **Visibility:** Do they know you?
- **Alignment:** Do they face the problem you solve?
- **Openness:** Are they innovation-friendly?

Color-code your sheet:

- **Red:** Cold zone (stay passive)
- **Yellow:** Warm zone (nurture)
- **Green:** Hot zone (take bold action)

Now your team knows where to direct their time and energy.

Sample Heat Map Table:

Department	Visibility	Alignment	Openness	Score (30)	Action
Health (MP)	8	9	6	23	Send model + impact study
Education (UP)	2	7	8	17	Introduce via workshop

Step 3: Create a Relationship Funnel

A dynamic funnel prevents leads from getting cold.

Think of it like a conversion funnel:

- **Stage 1:** Introduced → Added on WhatsApp/email list
- **Stage 2:** Engaged → Attended webinar/demo or requested info

- **Stage 3:** Interested → Had a meeting or requested a pilot
- **Stage 4:** Partnering → Issued letter, initiated MoU, or funded pilot

Your goal is to keep people moving across stages. No stagnation.

Create this funnel monthly:

- Measure % moved to next stage
- Track the average time spent in each stage
- Set a reminder to nudge stalled profiles

Step 4: Calendarize Engagement

The government runs on routine. Align your communication rhythm accordingly.

Here's a sample monthly planner:

- **Week 1:** Share a relevant government success case
- **Week 2:** Call follow-up to check implementation feedback
- **Week 3:** Invite to the insight session
- **Week 4:** Send birthday/anniversary/transfer update if applicable

These touches signal sincerity, not sales.

"You become memorable not by being loud, but by being consistent."

Use platforms like WhatsApp Business Broadcast, Mailchimp, and Calendly for automation.

Step 5: Build a Dashboard of Results, Not Just Contacts

Visibility without results leads to fatigue. Your dashboard must showcase real traction:

Track:

- Departments where you're on file (as an empaneled partner)
- Total govt meetings this quarter
- Sanctions or pilots initiated
- Testimonials received
- Number of recurring state engagements

Then segment them:

- By district/state
- By ministry
- By the pilot stage

Use a dashboarding tool that your team updates weekly. This becomes your war room.

Suggested Tools:

- Google Sheets with conditional formatting
- Airtable for relational dashboards
- Zoho CRM with Government Custom Tags

BONUS: Dashboard Pitfalls to Avoid

1. **Overloading with Data:** Simplicity wins. Focus on metrics that drive action.
2. **Static Tracking:** Your dashboard must evolve. New officials, new policies, new zones.
3. **Single Owner Syndrome:** Make it collaborative, not founder-dependent.
4. **Lack of Privacy Compliance:** Use ethical means to store officer data.
5. **Not Reviewing:** Hold a dashboard review meeting monthly.

Your Relationship System Is Your Real Asset

You can't scale a trust-based business on memory.

Build a living system that:

- Predicts opportunities before others see them
- Shows legitimacy without asking for it
- Converts interest into implementation
- Builds trust without crossing ethical lines

"If your contacts are a list, you're an amateur. If your contacts are a system, you're a force."

This chapter gives you the tools to be that force.

Chapter 11

COMPLIANCE WITHOUT COMPLEXITY

Staying Clean While Playing Big

Clean is Not Just Ethical, It's Strategic

When people hear "government business," one of the first concerns that arises is compliance. Many assume that working ethically with the government is slow, bureaucratic, and ultimately fruitless without bending the rules. This couldn't be further from the truth. In today's India, compliance is no longer a bottleneck—it's your strategic moat.

This chapter will break the myth that clean dealings limit scale. In fact, we'll show how structured compliance can protect your business, accelerate trust with decision-makers, and make your offering scalable across departments and states.

Compliance is Your Competitive Advantage

Why Do Ethical Businesses Win?

- Clean companies leave paper trails that officers can trust.
- When everything is documented, officers feel secure moving forward.

- In today's audit-heavy ecosystem (RTI, Vigilance, CAG), officers prefer vendors who know their way around documentation.

Strategic Trust Is Built on Compliance: Officers often want to say yes, but fear repercussions. When your business practices are transparent, you eliminate the fear factor.

Three Levels of Compliance to Win Trust:

- **Level 1:** Legal & Entity Level – GST, PAN, MoA, MSME, DPIIT Startup Certificate, FCRA (if required)
- **Level 2:** Proposal & Project Level – Clear MoUs, NDAs, Pilot Agreements, Co-funding terms, Result Frameworks
- **Level 3:** Impact & Audit Level – Data documentation, officer endorsements, quarterly reports, testimonials

Essential Documents That Build Credibility

Build and maintain a library of ready-to-use documents:

- Incorporation Certificate & GSTIN
- MSME Udyam Registration
- Startup India Recognition Certificate
- CSR Eligibility Letter (Section 135 compliant if NGO)
- Legal MoU Templates
- Pilot Proposal Format
- Post-Pilot Report Templates
- RTI-Ready Documentation Folder (photos, attendance sheets, before-after metrics)

When these are structured and available, you're seen as professional and reliable.

MoUs: The Strategic Gateway

Why MoUs Matter:

- They provide officers a safe way to test your idea
- They signal seriousness on both sides
- They become proof of precedent when expanding to other departments

Key Elements of a Strategic MoU:

- Purpose & Scope
- Pilot Duration and Departmental Role
- Deliverables and Output Metrics
- Legal Compliance Clauses
- Exit Clause (for non-performance)

Best Practices:

- Keep it lean (2-3 pages max)
- Avoid language implying permanent commitment
- Use performance-linked clauses (e.g., "If KPI met, project may be extended")

Audit-Proofing Your Impact

The government works on proof. Officers are held accountable. To scale, you must learn to present your work in an audit-proof way.

What Officers Look For:

- Beneficiary lists
- Photos with geotags
- Attendance with IDs
- Baseline vs. Endline metrics
- Third-party validation (if possible)

Toolkits to Maintain:

- **Impact Report Builder:** Automates data into a presentable PDF
- **Beneficiary Impact Form:** Digital or physical
- **Before-After Analysis Template:** For visible interventions

Make officers look good. They'll champion your cause internally.

RTI and Vigilance-Proof Processes

Your documents should survive RTI and internal audits.

How to Stay RTI-Proof:

- Share only what's necessary
- Never exaggerate impact
- Always link data to source files

Vigilance-Proof Strategy:

- Avoid undue advance payments
- Use email over WhatsApp
- Keep signed copies of everything

Your clarity gives comfort to the system.

Digital Compliance Infrastructure

Set up a simple digital structure that automates and stores your compliance:

- Google Drive Folder Hierarchy:
  - Entity Documents
  - Proposal Templates
  - MoU Copies
  - Pilot Reports
  - Testimonials
  - Photos & Media
- CRM System or Excel Tracker:
  - Officer name, department, region
  - Follow-ups & engagement stages
  - MoU dates & renewal timelines

This becomes your institutional memory.

Internal Compliance Team (Even if You're Small)

Even if you're a 5-person team, assign one person to:

- Maintain the compliance folder
- Handle officer follow-ups
- Send polite nudges for acknowledgements
- Draft MoUs or seek legal help

Train them on:

- Government language & protocols
- Drafting clean proposals
- Creating impact evidence

They are your silent scale enablers.

Scaling Compliance Across States

Once your systems are tested in one department, you can replicate them:

- Same MoU format with state customizations
- Case studies from past pilots
- Testimonials from officers to build instant trust

Use compliance to fast-track approvals:

- Officers share successful documents internally
- Peer departments replicate when there is no risk

The Role of Legal Advisors

Don't cut corners. Use expert legal help:

- For MoU vetting
- For partner agreements
- For CSR fund routing
- For RTI and FCRA regulations

Good legal help prevents bad headlines.

Turning Compliance into Brand Power

Promote your compliance culture in the right way:

- Mention it in pitch decks
- Share impact reports on LinkedIn
- Publish your templates for other startups

When you become an example of clean scaling, more doors open.

Chapter 12

Your Strategic Government Growth Plan: Integrating Everything

You've come this far. Now it's time to connect all the dots: offer, credibility, access, funding, relationships, dashboards, and compliance into one unified roadmap.

A **Strategic Government Growth Plan (SGGP)** is your customized blueprint for predictable, ethical, and scalable growth through government channels. Here is your step-by-step roadmap.

1. Define Your End Goals — Strategic Positioning First

Instead of blindly chasing tenders, define:

- What government challenges does your business solve?
- Which departments align most with your vision?
- What's the 3-year revenue goal from government verticals?
- What kind of impact do you want to be known for?

With clarity on purpose, everything else becomes measurable.

2. Map Your Strategic Footprint

Using your learnings from previous chapters, draw your SGGP map:

Phase 1 – Visibility:

- Publish 3 authority-building posts on LinkedIn
- Create 2 case studies with government results
- Upload MSME/Udyam/Startup India certifications

Phase 2 – Pilot Penetration:

- Identify 3 departments in one district/state
- Offer a free or co-funded pilot for proof-of-impact
- Collect feedback and a recommendation letter

Phase 3 – Scaling Systems:

- Automate dashboards, compliance folders, and team protocols
- Deploy fund rotation models to stay liquid
- Train second-in-line team leaders to replicate models

Phase 4 – National Expansion:

- Replicate models in 3 other states with similar departments
- Onboard retired government officials as advisors
- Integrate feedback loops and PR systems

3. Build Your Strategic Team

Your team is your asset.

Build three levels:

- **Execution Team:** field staff, project managers, admin support
- **Strategy Circle:** compliance expert, legal advisor, core consultant
- **Advocacy Allies:** retired officers, CSR heads, fund managers

Hold a monthly mission meeting where all 3 tiers review progress.

4. Use a Strategic Scorecard

Monitor progress with key metrics:

Metric	Monthly Target	Actual	Notes
No. of Government Meetings	5		
New Pilot Proposals Submitted	2		
MoUs Signed	1		
Feedback Letters Received	2		
Revenue Collected (Gov Sector)	₹		
New Contacts Added to Dashboard	10		

Keep this updated in your dashboard and review weekly.

5. Your Strategic Rituals: Rhythm Brings Results

Successful SGGPs aren't built in bursts; they're nurtured with rhythm:

- **Weekly:** Strategic call with consultant/mentor
- **Monthly:** District-level review of activities
- **Quarterly:** Publish 1 report or insight from your pilot
- **Yearly:** Host a "Gov Impact Roundtable" for departments

"The government doesn't trust fast talkers. It trusts consistent walkers."

6. Plug In the Growth Flywheel

Here's how your government business should start running like a flywheel:

1. ✅ Start small with a proof-based pilot
2. ✅ Collect data + testimonials
3. ✅ Use those to pitch bigger projects
4. ✅ Win more trust = more access
5. ✅ Scale geography + departments
6. ✅ Reinvest → expand team & reputation
7. ✅ Attract bigger govt/CSR collaborations
8. ✅ Build legacy with long-term MoUs

Your Masterplan in Motion & Final Words from the Author

The Strategic Government Growth Plan is your final transformation step. It's not theory, it's your **engine of ethical**

expansion. Done right, this becomes your business's most reliable, high-impact vertical.

The Government is not a black box. It's a massive engine looking for people like you: solvers, creators, impact builders. The old ways of manipulation and blind bidding are fading. A new generation of ethical entrepreneurs is stepping in.

If this book helped shift your mindset and gave you practical tools, then its mission is complete.

❌ Don't chase tenders. Align with strategy.

❌ Don't sell. Solve.

❌ Don't wait. Win.

Let's create ethical, massive business growth, with the government, not against it.

Let's co-create India's future, one department at a time.

See you in the field.

Dr. Anujj K Jain